GET THE CAREER YOU DESERVE

Set Goals, Find a Job and Get Paid What You're Worth!

I0484422

Phil Johnson

Copyright © 2015 by D/O Publishing

Introduction

So if you picked up this book, you're in need of a new job or career, am I right? While times have changed, the human condition always seems to stay the same. Working conditions have gotten much better over the last 100 years, but we still work jobs we loathe to put dinner on the table. How sad is that?

It's amazing really. People say there aren't a lot of jobs out there, but yet I go onto the internet and see hundreds of thousands of jobs available at my fingertips (results may vary).The problem is we either think we're not good enough for the job or that we're so comfortable with an uncomfortable lifestyle, that we're not willing to change because there's a chance something could go wrong.

Most of us tend to be paralyzed by fear. There's a fear of not knowing what will happen if you walk away from your job. How terrible would it be if you left the job you're with right now, cut ties to the biweekly paychecks, drove to another place of work and took a chance for more money… Money that makes you happy because you're doing a job that makes you happy?

Life is all about risk but yet no one wants to chance it. What if you fail? You lose what you have and are forced to start over? The question should be more "what if you succeed?"

Recently I was watching a video of the hilarious Jim Carrey giving a speech to a graduating class. Inspire all of the butt talking and craziness he's expressed in his Hollywood movies over the last 20+ years, he said something that truly hit home,:

"My father could have been a great comedian, but he didn't believe that was possible for him, and so he made a conservative choice. Instead, he got a safe job as an accountant, and when I was 12 years old, he was let go from that safe job, and our family had to do whatever we could to survive.

I learned many great lessons from my father, not the least of which was that you can fail at what you don't want, so you might as well take a chance on doing what you love."

-Jim Carrey, Commencement Address at the 2014 MUM Graduation

Being safe won't make you happy. In this book, we're going to explore what it is that truly makes you happy and then build you up into a brand that anyone can get behind and hire. You have to be willing to take chances. It's a competitive world out there and in order to survive, you have to stand out and be strong.

We'll self-analyze your current situation, we'll set a goal, make or revise your resume, use effective tools to find jobs, explore the options of using a temp agency, building a brand, connecting with people you know on the inside, and finish off with interviewing!

Chapter 1: Self Analyze

I'd like to think this is the easiest step in the entire process because who knows you better than yourself? You've been with yourself from the very beginning. Ironically, most people tense up and have no idea how to look at themselves with an objective mind. How can you expect to sell a company on you if you can't talk about you?

Look at yourself and try to break this down in real time. I'll use myself as an example as we put together a list. That's right… a LIST. Bust out a pen and paper and let's analyze.

What are your skills?

- Great at providing Customer Service
- Have awesome time management skills
- Great at over the phone sales
- Great at in-person sales
- Have experience handling large amounts of cash
- Extensive knowledge in Microsoft Office and Apple's iWork
- Extensive knowledge in Mac and Window PC environments
- Clean driving record
- Great at building work relationships
- Management experience
- Experience in Foodservice
- Experience at Training staff
- Guitar and singing
- Music Production
- Songwriting
- Conflict Management

No skill should be left off the list! Even if it isn't relevant to the job, you think you have in mind. You never know what kind of job could require a skill of yours. There is a time and place for every skill, and you may not want to lead with certain skills over others, but we'll discuss that later.

Now take a look at that list and put a checkmark next to the ones you actually like doing. Just because you're good at it doesn't mean you should do it. When I was in my late teens, I worked in a restaurant, and I HATED waiting on tables. Sure, I made a lot of money doing it, but it was by far the worst job I had.

My father is really good at drywall but if he had the choice between playing drums in a band and doing drywall, he'd hand up his drywall cape in a second.

What skills do I like doing/using:

- Customer Service
- Time management

- In-person sales
- Handling cash
- Mac and PC
- Management
- Training staff
- Guitar and Singing
- Music Production
- Songwriting

Look at your list and think about the reasons you like what you've picked. I personally love helping people! I love being on time, I like to be face to face with people, I don't mind handling large amounts of cash, I love working on computers, I like managing and training people, and I would love to have a job doing music!

The skills I've listed clearly won't always match each other, but we can use this list in a bit when we set up your resume.

Now let's write another list. I imagine this list is going to be a lot longer. Let's write down all the things you DON'T like doing. This will help us when it comes to picking out potential jobs.

What DON'T I want to do?

- Clean
- Drive
- Travel
- Policeman
- Security
- Cooking
- Talk on the phone
- Work with all men
- Overnight shift
- Work weekends
- Work more than 40 hours

The things you choose don't have to be super complicated. Sometimes one word can cover a whole lot of ground. For example, "clean" on my list means any type of scrubbing, taking out the garbage, cleaning toilets or any other miscellaneous thing that involves the act of cleaning. I feel I have enough skills to warrant a job that keeps me from doing that. Plus, I have a terrible eye for detail when it comes to cleaning.

Keep your lists close! We'll need them very soon!

Chapter 2: Set a Goal

If you're currently jobless or in a job you can't stand, you need to know truly what it is you want before you can go looking for it. First off, you'll waste a lot of time looking through endless job listings that will have no relation to what it is you truly want.

Setting goals are a great way to measure yourself in life, and you should do it in all aspects of your day from your life in general to your job.

How MUCH?

So before we talk about careers, let's figure out a real number that you need in order to be happy. Don't cop out with a simple answer like "a million dollars." Sure, that would be great, but unless you're already a position of power, it's highly unlikely you're going to find those kind of jobs laying around.

In order to figure out a real number, you need to look at your expensed first. So I'll use a list, for example:

Monthly Expenditures			
Rent	$600		
Renter's Insurance	$35		
Car payment	$355		
Car Insurance	$100		
Utilities	$230		
Credit Cards	$350	Total Debt	
Student Loans	$420	Estimated bills for Year	$30600
Food	$300		
Cable/Internet	$80		
Phone	$80		
Total	$2550		

So in this list, I broke down all the bills I have to pay out and on the right; I added all of that up. So if I don't calculate in any money for extra stuff outside of my normal living expenses, I'm going to need to make $30,600 after taxes.

If you live in the US, we are now required to have Health Insurance, which can add a bit more. I was lucky enough to work at a company who takes my insurance out before they tax me for it. My expenditures have made it necessary for me to make at LEAST $50k. That's to get a semi-social life and have decent health coverage. Pretty scary that I've let my life be dictated by this amount of money.

Let's make a list of things that you want to spend your money on. These will be the extra events and possessions that give you a life worth living!

Monthly Expenditures			
Date nights	$200		
Drinks with friends	$150		
Hobby/memberships	$200	Total for the year	$11400
Occasional possessions	$300		
Savings	$100		
Total per Month	$950		

Now we have a better idea of what it would take to be happy with our income. In this case, both expenditure totals add up to $42,000. Let's add 30% to that to account for health insurance and taxes which equals $54,600.

So in my case, the happy number would be $54,600 to pay for my bills, give me a social life, pay for insurance and put money away. I like to keep things clean so let's round up to $55k or give yourself a little breathing room and ask for $60k.

WHAT HOURS?

Now that we know how much we want to make, we have a big undertaking to figure out what our hourly limit will be to get it! My wife sells cars and puts in over 55 hours a week to get $60k a year. She's fully on commission, so no overtime is earned. There are many people who put in the same amount of hours and make far less.

How important is your time? Only you can truly make that decision. When it comes time to accept an offer, you decide what your time is worth at that very moment. When you're a teenager, any kind of money is worth your time. I remember the days where making 7.25 an hour was awesome. But back then I didn't have bills.

When I was 17, I made $10 an hour scooping ice-cream as an assistant manager. Back then, I saw myself as a high roller. My dad had his own drywall business, and he was paying his workers 10 dollars an hour. I made as much as them and did 1/10th the work! Pretty amazing stuff.

Once I got to college, I started teaching Guitar for $20 an hour. I only taught 6 hours a week... so that didn't amount to the 40-hour work week total of most jobs.

Generally, if I'm working for someone else, I don't want to spend more than 40 hours a week there. Only in rare circumstances will I extend my stay, but it is more the exception to the rule than a rule itself.

Once you figure out the total you're willing to work for, you have to decide what time of day you're willing to work. 9-5? 3 PM- 3AM? Overnight shift? There are some added bonuses to some.

I always liked the 9-5 shift because it's essentially the closest thing to the way children are raised to be away from home. As a child, we go to school five days a week, 8-4. Then when we get home, we have free time.

Depending where you live, sometimes that shift can be a crap because you have to fight the morning and afternoon commute. That can tack on an hour or two extra to your day that you're not getting paid for.

Working a twilight shift that takes place from 3 PM - 3 AM can be liberating. You get to sleep in as late as you want, and you'll usually avoid most day-to-day traffic problems. The beginning of your shift might be slightly hectic depending on the job, but it usually relaxes in the wee hours of the night.

Overnight shifts have a fair share of both pros and cons. The pros are that in most states, you're supposed to be paid a 10% premium over a person who works a day shift. Your schedule usually doesn't change too rapidly because most businesses want you to have a decent quality of life. Sometimes you're given the opportunity to work extra hours in a night so that you can get three days off a week instead of the normal 2. The commute is the easiest drive of them all.

The cons can make working overnight are tricky. Sadly you are living the opposite of the world. You're asleep when all the good things happen (everybody's awake during the day). You have to be strategic about how you plan your days to hang out with people, taking into account that you may be exhausted as hell. If there is ever a buffet meal given to your place of employment, overnight usually gets the short end of the stick. (Clearly I'm speaking from personal preference).

If I'm going Salary, I can't make less than $60k a year. If I'm working by hourly, that comes out to roughly $29 an hour. What's your rate?

What Type of Job Do You Want?

This is a loaded question. I always wanted to be a rockstar! Sadly, there aren't any companies that are offering that right now. So I look to my list that I wrote down earlier. I have an interest in Face-to-Face selling. I am skilled in computers and musical pieces, and I don't mind handling big money.

Unless I'm the manager of a Guitar Center, there's no way I'm getting $60k a year. But I'll keep an eye out for that job just in case. The point is the skills you like using will determine what kind of job you can have.

Write down a list of places or types of jobs you wouldn't mind working.

Where Job Would I like to Work?
Computer sales
Car Sales
Teaching
Bank
Music School

Keep that list! We have a use for it!

Chapter 3: Resume Basics!

Now that we have a list of jobs that you wouldn't mind working, this is our chance to make a resume that will focus on the skills relevant to that job. I'm not sure a bank would be very interested in my ability to play guitar and sing, just as a Music School wouldn't be interested if I were a good Car salesman.

There are whole books dedicated to making the perfect resume, so we won't go too far into detail. We will focus on the general knowledge that will give you the ability to leverage your strengths to get the job you desire. If you need help building a resume, I will recommend the website howtowritearesume.net I used them a few years ago, it formatted my resume, and I was happy. Plus, it will help you get your thoughts organized.

Before we go into writing the resume, you need to do an inventory of every job you've ever had. It doesn't matter how grand or stupid it was, write each of them down on a word processor and leave a few spaces under each.

Now write what your responsibilities were for each of those, and talk about some skills you flexed in the position.

Jerry's Ice-Cream
Managed a team of 8 employees to run the day to day operations of the store.
Handled up to $10,000 of cash with store closings
Extensive experience ordering products for the store on a weekly basis
Trained all new employees which led to the leading Ice Cream store in the region

Guitar Teacher
Handled a studio of 14 students ranging from all levels.
Had a retention rate of 85%

And so on and so forth. It's important to note all of the achievements! You never know what may stick out to an employer.

Once you've written them all, It's time to look at each type of job you'd be interested in applying for, and create a resume with the positions that hold relevance. The great part of a website like howtowritearesume.net is that they let you make different versions.

Chapter 4: Build Your Brand

Before we go submitting our resumes to a bunch of random companies, we need to make sure that you have made yourself a brand.

I recommend you create an account at linkedin.com This website is like the professional networking version of Facebook. You put down all the jobs you've worked; people endorse you for skills based on their experience working with you. Some websites will allow you to use your LinkedIn profile like a resume.

While in the process of building your brand, you must also clean up anything that could potentially bring your chances of getting a job any harm.

FACEBOOK

Facebook is a great website. You get to stay connected to people all over the world and stay clued in on what everybody's doing all the time. It's also become an online journal for most, because it keeps pictures of everything from your past including the parties where you got wasted, your drunken status posts, the inappropriate jokes you shared with the world... You get the picture.

You have got to do some clean up on any social media profile. It's almost a certainty that if a company is interested in hiring you, they are going to look you up and see if you're the type of candidate they're looking for. You passed out on a beer pong table will only burn an image into their mind that will have them staying far away from you when it comes time to hiring.

Cover Photo

If you have some money laying around, or a friend that has an iPhone, get a professional picture of yourself taken. Or what we like to call a 'headshot.' Something with you smiling wearing something professional can be a nice touch to whatever profiles you have up online when the companies begin their search on you.

If you look scary and intimidating, there may be a reason to skip over you. Be presentable and look professional.

REACH OUT

It's very important that when you're about to start looking for a job, that you make a list of friends that work at the type of places you're interested in and reach out for advice, help, or a backdoor way to getting a job. I probably say this in every single one of my books, but it's not what you know, but who you know.

Believe it or not, most companies would rather hire somebody who is known by somebody on the inside before hiring blindly. They know they can trust you (especially if they trust the person whose recommending you,) and they have someone to blame if that person messes up... Just kidding... but maybe not really.

The great part about linkedin.com is that it has a collection of all your friends, the jobs that they have held or are currently in, and the skills that each of them has, and it lays it right in front of you. You don't have to dig far to figure out who you want in your corner. Sometimes that's the first place to start when looking for a job! Some companies will let employees know that they'll be looking for a new member and if they have anyone to suggest before they post the listing to bring them in. Never underestimate the power of friendship!

Chapter 5: Find Job Listings

Now that you have a resume, an idea of what type of jobs you want to work and an income goal, we can now go job hunting. Back in the old days, we would have to grab a newspaper, look who was hiring and then go down to the business and apply. Everybody had to do it. With the internet, so many people are instructed to apply online. Ironically, going into a store gives you a better chance of getting a name to the face with the employer which could up your chances.

We'll go through a list of websites you can use in your career search. Of course, there are many others but it can't hurt to get started with any of these companies.

Craigslist

This probably wasn't the first thing you had on your mind. Craigslist is like the poor man's eBay. There are no fees to use them, and you can find a plethora of things in your local area from pets, dates, instruments and you guessed it; jobs.

In many cases, Craigslist is a better place to look than your local newspaper. There are usually hundreds of postings based on where you live. You can find anything from short gigs where you can make a quick buck, to jobs that pay under the table, to hidden gems. Usually, you won't find high paying jobs on Craigslist. They'll usually pay a modest $0-$30k depending which job you get. There will be a lot of postings for personal escorts and other various oddball jobs that pay a lot.

I always check Craigslist first because it requires no personal information to look. However, I recommend you be wary when you do decide to apply for a job. There is a lot of spammers on Craigslist that tries to bait you in with a job and then will spam the hell out of you.

If a job sounds too good to be true, it most definitely is. You won't be the only one who sees it either. Be careful when giving out your information.

On the flip side, make sure you're not spamming a bunch of different jobs without seriously looking at the requirements. There's nothing more frustrating to a hiring manager than getting a bunch of non-relevant resumes. It wastes time, and it's very disrespectful

Careerbuilder and Monster

I group these together because they seem to be one and the same. The type of jobs that you'll generally find on here will be a bit larger in pay and very specialized.

You'll set up a profile and upload different versions of your resumes, and can post them for recruiters to find. I'm going to be honest with you. If you sign up with either of them, you're going to be invited by every insurance company in the land to work for them. Unless you have a true passion for sales, I don't recommend you do this. They'll bait you with attractive compensation, but you'll soon find out you'll be paying yourself all of those... plus it's soul-sucking.

What I do like about both tools is that they will allow you to determine what kind of jobs you want to be alerted for. Aren't you glad we did the exercise already so you know exactly what you're looking for?

indeed.com

Indeed has a mixture of low-end and high-end jobs. I like this site a lot because it isn't very intrusive. It's like a search engine for jobs. It's very basic when it comes to graphics, but it lets your search for jobs based on place and distance. There will be 2 or 3 advertised jobs at the top and bottom, but you'll generally find a lot of good jobs through the site.

snagajob.com

Snagajob is like the minimum wage job fair. It's very rare you'll find a job that pays much more than the bare minimum. You'll usually find a lot of fast food places on there, department stores, and other big box chains. If you're looking for a temporary job to make small bucks, snag will be a good place to look, but if you're looking for something more, I highly recommend the others above.

Temp Agency

While searching for a job can be fun in its' own right, it can be a lot easier having someone else hunting for jobs for you. A temp agency is essentially a company who hires people to work at jobs temporarily. Sometimes those jobs develop into careers... sometimes not.

I had a buddy of mine join a temp agency after one of his craigslist gigs fell through. He worked at a car factory making $15 doing a mindless job on a twilight shift. One day, he went to work without his Worker ID. They sent him home to go get it. He thought that was ridiculous, so he had another person swipe him in. Within minutes, he was fired.

The temp agency was given a letter of recommendation for him to work at another car factory because they had to fire him based on a technicality. He ended up getting a temp job at Mercedes-Benz. He worked there for three months and managed to save the company over a million dollars because it was able to reduce a process by a few extra steps. The company was thrilled, sent him to college to get his degree and is now making over $100k a year.

Since you know what you want in a job, it's easy to hand that over to an agency and have them find the job you're looking for.

Another bonus is some temp agencies will allow you to get benefits while you work under their umbrella.

Cover Letter

As we mentioned earlier, you want to make sure you use the right resume on the right company. Sadly, resumes aren't always as powerful by themselves anymore. It seems companies really want you to prove you want the job. That's where a cover letter comes in.

A Cover Letter is a 'letter' that you write to go along with your application materials with a personal message to the hiring manager. It can say something simple like what the contents of the application hold, as well as highlighting a few of your skills and your enthusiasm to work with them.

I don't recommend sending a generic cover letter because a gatekeeper can see them a mile away. It's very important that you look at key points in the job description and tie some of your skills to those.

For example

To Whom it May Concern,

Attached to this letter is my resume. As you will see, I have experience teaching students and have a great teacher-student relationship skill based on my 85% retention rate. I believe that the skills I have detailed will be a great asset to your company. You can contact me at 555-5609 if you'd like to set up an interview to discuss this opportunity further.

Thanks and good luck on your search

Phil Johnson

It doesn't have to be anything crazy, but if you relate your strengths to their needs, you'll already be 90% ahead of the competition.

While the internet is a wonderful way to find jobs, unless it's specifically noted, do try to get some face time with the company. Apply inside and ask questions.

Apply

Now you have your list of jobs, resumes, and cover letters; it's time to apply! Don't put all your eggs and one basket and apply to one place. You'll have a higher chance of failure. The more applications you have flying around, the better chance you'll get a callback.

If you can, dedicate one of your days off to just applying. Get up early (before the competition) and get to it!

A few years ago, I applied to a huge sales company at 3 in the morning. I was up late; I didn't get up early. I sent in my application, took the tests they required and went to bed. At 8 AM the following morning, their NEW hiring manager started and I was the very first applicant she had seen based on the time I applied. She called me in for an interview, and I was working three days later.

Every morning, check your usual job listing sites and apply there. There are always a handful of new jobs. Check at night too if you can!

If you are offered an interview with a job you're not interested in, TAKE THE INTERVIEW. Interview practice can be a very valuable thing during the job hunting process. You get an opportunity to see what works and what doesn't. If you're successful and start getting job offers, it can add to your confidence and make you do even better in an interview that counts. Besides, it may lead to a job you didn't think you'd ever go for, and it may pay for more than what you need.

Now that you've submitted your resume and material, within a few days, you'll get a phone call from a job that you're interested in. Let's set you up for success!

Chapter 6: The Interview

Growing up, I was always told that first impressions will make or break an interaction. If you come off as a preverbal douchebag, there's a chance that person will never want to see you again. On the flip side, if you're easy to talk to, motivated and have a fun sense about you, it could make you so infectious that they want to keep hanging around you.

A job interview is a chance to see which category you will fall into. There are many ways that you're going to prove you are right for the job, but the most important part is prepare yourself both emotionally as well as have answers at the ready so that if you're asked some of these basic questions blindly, you're not caught off guard and found mumbling like an idiot.

Make Your Own Elevator Pitch

Right now, your resume and cover letter are the only things that the hiring manager has in front of them to base wanting a working a relationship with you. Sometimes paper just doesn't do justice. Sometimes you'll find that when you go in for an interview, they never even looked at your resume. I've had that happen dozens of times. The hiring manager looks around for my resume, and he can't find it. I hand him an extra resume, and he sets it aside and continues to question.

Usually, one of the first (or last) questions a manager will ask is "Why do you think you'd be a good fit?" There are various ways to ask that question, but they all rely on your answer being an elevator pitch.

An elevator pitch is a short 30 second to a minute description to sell yourself. Not every elevator pitch can be the same for every job you're applying for. Like your resume, you want to tie specific skills to the specific needs of the business that you're applying for.

It should be easy to create on the account that you have a list of skills written down somewhere.

"Well Steve, I've been in sales for over ten years beating sales forecasts time and time again, all while training a complete sales team to do the same. I have a true passion for helping people but also a passion for bettering myself. I feel here at XXX I can flex those muscles and take myself to an even higher level."

Short and sweet. I highlighted a couple things from my resume, but I say it with confidence. Don't lie to them. Focus on what you're most confident about. Confidence can do wonders in an interview!

General Interview questions you need to be ready for

Here we're going to go through a list of questions that you'll almost always have to answer in an interview. It's important that you practice answer for these because it will give you confidence when you answer them, but it will also reaffirm what you should already know!

1. What is your greatest strength?

Here, you want to pick a strength that will resonate heavily with the company you're interviewing for:

"My greatest strength is my ability to connect with people. In every job I've ever had, whether it was by survey or a compliment to my manager, I've been applauded for building relationships with customers and making them feel comfortable."

2. What is your greatest weakness?

You want to be careful how you answer this. Don't focus on the negative aspects but rather on the positive. If you're going to name a weakness, make sure it's something that isn't needed in the job you're interviewing for. On the flip side, if your greatest weakness is a core skill for the job, talk about how you've improved it from coming from your last job.

"Sometimes my ability to get things done on time and most cases early can get a little crazy because I hate to be late."

3. Tell us about a time where you were faced with an obstacle and how you overcame it.

With these type of open-ended questions, they are looking to see you talk negatively about a situation. You need to make sure when you're asked these kind of questions, which you focus only on the positive. Keep the answer concise and to the point.

"On a product launch day, one of our manager's had quit his position. He was one of two managers for the day, and because I had the most knowledge of the managerial base, I managed to step up and help with processes that made the day run by smoothly."

4. How do you handle success?

A lot of interviewers will focus on questions that will pull you one way and then pull you another. We're always waiting for a reason to explain why we are better than the terrible situation they're asking about, but be ready for the positives.

"Personally, If I have success in a situation, I want to teach it out to my team. When I identify the skills, it takes to be successful, I try to scale up and give my teammates success. We are only as strong as our weakest man."

5. How do you handle failure?

This is one of those questions where they want to see how resilient you are. Do you just give up and die? Or do you learn something from it?

"Failure is just another step I have to take to get to success. If I'm unsuccessful at something, I seek feedback, set short term goals for myself and work towards it until I am successful. I don't believe in giving up, and there is always room for improvement."

6. Have you ever had a tough conversation with a co-worker? If so, how did it take place?

This is the type of question that will look for your conflict management skills. Are you overly emotional or do you approach challenges from a calm place.

"I had a co-worker who was constantly late with no regard for anybody else's time. People gave her feedback daily, but she didn't care. One day I asked her what her goals were in the company. She shared them with me, and I told her 'If you want to get there, you're going the support of the team. Right now, you don't have the support. I want to see you get there, but I can't help you if you won't help us.' After our heart to heart, she became much more punctual and eventually got the job she wanted... with support from the team.

7. Describe a time when you had to motivate your co-workers.

This kind of question is meant to see what extra skills you can bring to their current team.

"When I worked at an Ice-cream store, for every hour that we sold $800 of ice-cream, our store owner would put $20 in the tip jar. There were nine employees, so $20 didn't go that far. So I devised a plan with the shift leaders (I was assistant manager at the time). We assigned 5 people to make ice cream, one person to switch out empty ice cream barrels, one person to do dishes, one person to ring out ice cream at the register, and the final person to play games with the crowd to encourage more tipping. It became an assembly line, and we managed to hit the goal six times that day. Once we mastered it, I managed to implement it on busy days, and it brought a large influx of cash to the employee's hands and brought a higher morale to the store."

8. Why is there a gap between jobs?

If at any point during your adult years that you've had a gap in employment, you want to be sure you have a good reason. Living on unemployment isn't very exciting... Make sure to focus on developmental things... like classes, starting a business, etc.

"During the six months where I didn't have employment, I was in college finishing up my last semester of college. I wanted to make sure I had no distractions so that I could finish with a 4.0 GPA. As you'll see, right out of college I got a job and worked every moment from there."

9. What do you like to do outside of your job?

This gives the employer a little bit of insight what your interests are. It's important to highlight that you do have a life outside of your job. Who knows, you may have something in common that you can talk about with the interviewee.

"I like to write songs and play guitar on my own time. I have a recording studio and play weddings from time to time. I also like to write books for Kindle!"

10. What are your salary requirements?

This is important! You can't sell yourself short. You already know the number you need to be happy. Don't be afraid of making them uncomfortable. If they can't pay you that, then maybe you shouldn't be working there!

"Based on my experience and what I'll bring to your company, I feel $60,000 is a fair compensation that I require to be able to do this job."

Usually at the end of an interview they will ask if you have any questions. It's always important to ask what the "next steps" are. You need to know if they're looking to make a decision on the position sooner rather than later, or if they're planning on searching for a while to fill it. See if they will let you know either way. Some businesses won't take the time to let those who didn't get the job know.

Follow-Up

After a few days (a week or so) it's always fair to call and find out if a decision has been made. Even an email will suffice. You just want to show that you're interested and that you really want the job. Check back on a weekly to biweekly basis until they give you the final word. You don't want to pester them, but your time is valuable.

Job Offer

If you're offered a job and they offer less than what you requested, don't take it lying down. Stand behind what you're worth. If they lowball you severely, don't bother with them. If they offer you close to your number, try to negotiate. If it's a couple thousand dollars a year difference, see if there is a way to make it work. If you work hard, you'll be able to reach the total you want plus some after you move up in the company.

If they let you know you didn't get the position, don't fret. Ask if you could get some feedback from the interview and continue your search. You won't get every job you apply for. It's important to know that each of your failures will move you towards your success.

Conclusion

I'd like to personally thank you for reading this book. I always appreciate helping people that want to help themselves. This is a great step in trying to get the career you deserve. Analyzing your skills, setting goals, creating a resume, searching for a job, and interview is a normal process but you can get good at it. All the skills you learn in through that process can only help you as you grow in the company. Chances are you will have many interviews for positions you want.

It's important to know that there may be many jobs that you are qualified for, but sometimes you won't be the "perfect fit" that an employee is looking for. That's OK. There are many places that take their employee's happiness seriously, and there could be a chance your personality wouldn't mend well. Don't take it personally.

Never give up in the process and be hungry to learn every step of the way. Never settle for second best and strive to do what you want to do. Too many people live their lives working on something that doesn't fulfill their lives. Don't be that person. Life is fragile, and we don't get a lot of time to live it. Spend your time focused on the things that you love, with the people you love, and remember to do things for yourself every once in awhile.

Check out these other books brought to you by D/O PUBLISHING!

http://www.amazon.com/dp/B00U2WP4H0

STAY HUMAN: THE 8 STEPS TO BECOMING A SALES ROCKSTAR by **Phil Johnson**

STAY HUMAN: THE 8 STEPS TO BECOMING A SALES ROCKSTAR is a fantastic guide that will give you the tools you need to get started as a sales person

Are you new to sales? Are you having trouble hitting sales goal or making connections with your customers? You're not alone. There are a lot of sales people out there but for every good salesman there is, there 9 others that aren't. You don't have to be a part of that unskilled pool of talent.

In this book we'll go through 8 steps that will help analyze your interactions, give you tips and exercises to practice so that you'll be a top ranked salesperson in no time!

STAY HUMAN
The book focuses on taking the emphasis off selling a product and focusing on being genuine to build a connection

HOW TO NAVIGATE INTERACTIONS

We go through everything from the first impression to the final goodbye, setting you up for the best success!

DIFFERENT SCENARIOS
We break down different types of interactions and point at what to look for.

If you're just getting started, or need a fresher in the most practical sales techniques, look no further than STAY HUMAN: THE 8 STEPS TO BECOMING A SALES ROCKSTAR

HOW TO THINK LIKE A MILLIONAIRE: TIPS AND TRICKS TO BE MORE PRODUCTIVE AND MAKE BIG MONEY! By Phil Johnson

All we want is to be rich! We want enough money to pay for all of our desires and live a luxurious life with little to no effort. The sad part is that unless you win the lottery, or inherit some money from a wealthy relative, it's not just going to fall into your lap. You have to work for it!

Through out this book, we will explore the thinking of a millionaire and ways that you can adapt so that you can motivate yourself to become more!

We'll reference some of the world's most known millionaires (and some billionaires) while calling you to action to get up and change your life.

What are you waiting for?! Hit the download button now and change your mindset now!

http://www.amazon.com/dp/B00V1QANCW

http://www.amazon.com/dp/B00U5QA88S

WAKE UP AND GO! A GUIDE TO GET YOUR LIFE BACK by **Matthew Newton**

WAKE UP AND GO! A GUIDE TO GET YOUR LIFE BACK is all in the title. Are you caught in a rut? Feel like you're going in circles and never seem to find happiness? In this guide, we will break down whats pulling you down, and find new ways to rebuild yourself!

LOOK AT YOUR LIFE
We will analyze what's right in wrong at this current moment in time

LOOK AT YOUR LOVE LIFE
Whether you're in a relationship or not, we will get down to the fundamentals and find ways to revitalize your love life!

WHO DO YOU WANT TO BE?
We will take a look at all things that you dreamed of being but used excuses to avoid trying for.

DISCONNECT AND RECONNECT
We will cut ties with the ones the bring us down and we'll give you tips to reconnect with the "friends for a lifetime"

CAREER

We will analyze your job and career ambitions and find ways to improve them or start over all together!

STOP BUYING POSSESSIONS... MAKE MEMORIES

Instead of spending countless dollars on things that will ultimately never be used or break, we find a way to plan a trip of a life time.

AND SO MUCH MORE...

If you need help or guidance on what to do, read this book, do the exercises, and get your life back!

·

www.ingramcontent.com/pod-product-compliance
Lightning Source LLC
Chambersburg PA
CBHW070802180526
45168CB00004B/1720